Susanna Gretz & Alison Sage

teddybears
cookbook

illustrated by Susanna Gretz

Benn Book
COLLECTION

The Benn Book Collection
Published by Doubleday & Company Inc., Garden City, New York

Text & Illustrations Copyright © 1978 Ernest Benn Limited
All rights reserved

First edition in the United States of America
Printed in England

ISBN 0-385-13326 X (TRADE)
0-385-14415-6 (PREBOUND)
Library of Congress Catalog Card Number 77-747076

Library of Congress Cataloging in publication data.
Gretz, Susanna & Sage, Alison
Teddybears Cookbook.
"The Benn Book Collection"
Summary: Twenty-three easy-to-follow recipe treats including
snacks, salads, desserts, and drinks

[I. Cookery — Juvenile Literature]
[I. Cookery]
I. Title
TX652. 2G73 64 1.5 77-747076.

Recipes

Practical hints

Equivalents:

1 oz = 1 heaping tablespoon of flour
1 oz = 2 heaping tablespoons grated cheese
1 oz = 2 tablespoons butter or margarine

In these recipes, unless it says *heaping*, always use *level* spoonfuls.

Ovens:

Unless the recipe says otherwise, use the *middle* of the oven.
Always use potholders when handling hot dishes.
And remember that not only are things *in* the oven very hot, but things that have just come *out* of the oven can also burn you.
That includes food!

Dear Reader,

Bears are good at all sorts of things, but they especially like *cooking*. Even Fred likes to watch, although he really prefers the eating side of things. With a little practice, you can cook too. Just go slowly and carefully and remember these very important

Bear's words of advice:

1 Recipes where you will need to use the stove are marked 🐻 *Always* ask a friendly adult to help you when you use the stove, especially when you need to put things in or take them out of the oven or grill.
2 Wash your hands, clean off the table and put on an apron before you begin, because it is not a good idea to mix food with other things.
3 Read the whole recipe aloud first. This way, you can get everything you need ready before you start.
4 Take your time! If you rush about too fast, something is bound to spill or break.
5 Be careful with sharp knives. Leave heavy saucepans for adults and think twice about touching anything *hot*
6 Try to clear up as you go along, and then tidying up at the end is really not too bad, especially if everyone joins in and helps.

Have a good time cooking!

love

Charles

One morning there were five bears round a cookbook.

"It says here," said Charles, "that the first thing to learn is how to boil an egg."

"Then," said John. "We can make . . .

Colored eggs

1 egg for each person
saucepan of water
1 teaspoon of vinegar

Coloring

onion skins	golden yellow or brown eggs
blueberry or grape juice ⎫ beet ⎭	pale purple
3–4 drops of artificial food coloring	pink or rosy red
coffee grounds	coffee-colour
cold tea	pale brown

Take as many eggs as you have people and put them carefully in a saucepan of cold water. Now add the vinegar and the coloring of your choice. The more you add the darker the color will be.

Turn on the stove and put the saucepan on the heat. Leave for nine minutes. (This depends on how big and how fresh your eggs are, and also, of course, on how you like them cooked. Nine minutes will usually cook the white and leave the yolk runny.)

Take the eggs out of the saucepan, put them into egg cups and eat with salt and pepper.

Let's start now.

Cinnamon toast

For three bears (or people)

3 slices of bread
butter or margarine for spreading
$\frac{1}{2}$ teaspoon of ground cinnamon
2 tablespoons of soft brown sugar

If you don't like cinnamon, you could try

Buttered honey

Mix together the sugar and cinnamon in a small bowl. Then toast each slice of bread under the grill on one side only and spread the steamy, untoasted side with butter. Now sprinkle on your sugar and cinnamon mixture.

Next, put the toast back under the grill for a few minutes until the topping is golden brown and bubbling. Take it out and leave it on a plate for a few moments to cool.

Cut the toast up into small pieces and eat as quickly as you want to.

Simply mix together 4 tablespoons of butter or margarine with one (generous) tablespoon of honey. Now spread this mixture on your toast as before and grill.

Both mixtures burn very quickly, so remember to watch them carefully.

Kabobs and other prickly animals

For 4 people (Allow about 3 kabobs per person)

$\frac{1}{2}$ cabbage
cocktail sticks

Choose from:
4 cooked sausages
2 oz cheese
2 oz cooked chicken
2 oz cooked ham
2 tomatoes
1 green pepper
1 banana
1 small can of pineapple pieces
   (apricots or peaches are nice too)
$\frac{1}{2}$ cucumber
2 cooked potatoes
2 cooked carrots
1 stick of celery

First, get someone to help you look in
   the cupboard and decide exactly
   what you can use. Then lay
   everything out on a chopping board
   and cut it up into bite-sized pieces.
Next, thread the pieces onto cocktail
   sticks. Try to think of things that
   taste good and look pretty together.
   It's best to find what does both! It
   is a good idea to have something
   firm at each end (like a piece of
   cheese), to stop the pieces from
   slipping off the sticks.
Now stick your kabobs into the
   cabbage, and everyone can take a
   kabob when they want to.

Pigs in blankets

1 hot dog for each person
1 thin slice of bacon ⎫
1 heaping teaspoon of ⎬ for each
   grated cheese ⎭ hot dog
a pinch of pepper
some cocktail sticks

Oven setting:
  350°F

Turn on the oven.
Now cut a long slit lengthwise in each
  hot dog, and fill each slit with
  grated cheese. Next, cut the rind off
  the bacon, and wrap one slice
  snugly round each hot dog, making
  sure that it doesn't come undone
  by skewering it with a cocktail
  stick.
Add a little pepper.
Put the hot dogs in a shallow oven
  dish and put it in the oven for 10–12
  minutes, or until the cheese is all
  bubbly and the bacon is crisp.
Eat with a bun, or a slice of fresh
  bread.

Andrew says, these are very good for
supper, or (if you wait until they have
cooled down) for eating with your
fingers at a party.

The pig is the hotdog and the blanket is the bacon.

8

9

Green salad special

1 head of lettuce
1 apple
1 stick of celery
a few drops of lemon juice
a carton of cottage cheese (you could
   use ½ cup of grated cheese)

Wash the lettuce, drain it and break
   it up. Scrub the stick of celery, take
   off the leaves and chop it into little
   pieces. Remove the core of an apple
   (you may be lucky enough to find a
   special corer, otherwise use a knife)
   and chop it up into small pieces
   too. To keep the apple from going
   brown, sprinkle lemon juice on the
   pieces as soon as you have cut them
   up.
Arrange celery, apple and lettuce on a
   flat serving-dish and in the middle
   put the cottage cheese.

Charles says, instead of cheese, you
can use 2 hard-boiled eggs, cut into
quarters. The white and yellow of the
eggs looks very pretty with the green
lettuce. Other things you could use
are: Small slices of red and green
pepper, a few cooked peas, or slices of
tinned pineapple. In fact, try any
cooked or raw vegetable you like which
might be about. Nuts are nice, too.

Sara's salad dressing

Some people like salad dressing from a bottle; but it is great fun to try making your own.

1 pot of natural yoghurt
2 teaspoons of vinegar (wine vinegar is best)
a few drops of lemon juice
1 teaspoon of sugar
2 tablespoons of salad oil
pinch of salt and pepper to taste

Mix everything together in a bowl until it looks like rather runny mayonnaise.
Keep in a refrigerator.

11

Eggs in their nests

An egg for each person
   (or more, if they look hungry)
1 tablespoon cooked ham per person
1 teaspoon chopped parsley or herbs
   (if you like them)
1 teaspoon of cream per person
salt and pepper
1 teaspoon of butter per person

Oven setting:
   350°F

Turn on the oven.
Find some small, oven-proof bowls,
   one for each person, and rub them
   thickly inside with butter or
   margarine.
Now chop up the ham, mix it with
   herbs or parsley and share the
   mixture between each of the bowls.
   Break one egg (or more) carefully
   into each bowl and pour the cream
   on top. Sprinkle with a pinch of salt
   and a little pepper.
Then put the bowls on one oven tray.
   Put this into the oven for about 15
   minutes, or until the whites of the
   eggs look firm, but the yolks are
   still wobbly. They are now ready;
   take them out of the oven and eat
   quickly before they get cold.

Lunchtime..

Surprise eggs

Try using 1 tablespoon of grated cheese, cooked mushrooms, corn or chopped-up cooked sausage, or even a little chopped-up boiled potato instead of the ham.

Dog's dinner

4 medium potatoes
2 small onions
1 medium can of tomatoes (or 4 small fresh
    tomatoes)
$\frac{1}{2}$ cup peas (fresh or cooked)
1 level teaspoon of brown sugar
1 stock cube
1 large can of baked beans in tomato sauce
1 level teaspoon of mixed herbs
    (if you like them)
salt and pepper
2 oz butter cut into little pieces
2 oz grated cheese
Oven setting: 350°F

Put on the oven and get someone to help you
    open the cans.
Find a casserole, or a cooking pot with a lid.
Wash your potatoes and slice them thickly,
    cutting out any black marks.
Next peel and slice the onions.
Now put two or three pieces of butter in the
    casserole or pot and then put in layers of
    onion, tomato, beans, potato, and peas.
Next, add a *little* salt and pepper, and the
    herbs. Repeat the layers until you almost fill
    the pot. Save a few slices of potato to put on
    the top and finally dot with the remaining
    butter and the grated cheese.
Crumble a stock cube into $\frac{1}{2}$ pint of hot water,
    add the sugar and pour this mixture over
    your casserole.
Now put on the lid, and put the pot in the oven
    for $1\frac{1}{2}$ hours, or until it is cooked. If you like
    the topping crunchy, get someone to take
    off the lid for the last 10 minutes.

14

Honey-baked bananas

1 ripe banana for each bear
1 teaspoon of soft
  brown sugar
1 teaspoon of honey
  (runny honey is best) } for each banana
a teaspoon of butter for each banana,
  plus extra for the dish
a few drops of lemon juice

Oven setting:
350°F

Put on the oven.
Find an oven-proof dish and rub it
  thickly with butter or margarine.
  Then peel each of the bananas and
  put them in it.
Next pour a few drops of lemon juice
  over them. Now spread them with
  honey and sprinkle over the brown
  sugar.
Finally, dot them with the butter and
  put the dish in the oven for about
  15 minutes, or until the bananas are
  a creamy, toffee color.
Serve with ice cream, or just on their
  own.

15

Brown Betty

4 oz margarine or butter
3 cups bread crumbs
$\frac{2}{3}$ cup soft brown sugar
$1\frac{1}{2}$ lb apples
$\frac{1}{2}$ lemon
pinch of cinnamon (if you like it)
$\frac{1}{2}$ pint of warm water

Oven setting:
  350°F

Put on the oven.

Cut up the margarine or butter, put it into an oven-proof dish with the bread crumbs. Then put the dish in the oven for about 10 minutes, or until the butter has melted and the bread crumbs are starting to go brown. Take out the dish.

Peel, core and slice the apples and put them in a bowl of cold water until you need them. Grate the yellow part of the lemon rind. Now put a layer of sliced apple on the bottom of a deep pie dish. Sprinkle over a layer of bread crumbs and a little of the lemon rind. Then put in another layer of apple. Go on putting in layers until your dish is full, ending up with a thick layer of bread crumbs.

Next, add the cinnamon, sugar and juice from the lemon to the water and then pour it over the mixture in the pie dish.

Dot the top of the bread crumbs with a little extra butter. (This will give you a buttery, crunchy topping.)

Put in the oven and bake for 1 hour or until apples are soft.

Serve with ice cream or custard.

Apple snow with a kiss

3 egg whites
2 tablespoons of sugar
$\frac{1}{2}$ lemon
$\frac{1}{2}$ pint of sweetened apple sauce
red jam

Mix the apple sauce with the juice of half a lemon.
Now whisk the egg whites in another bowl until they are stiff and foamy. A good test is when the mixture stands in stiff peaks.
Stir the sugar gently into the egg white little by little and then carefully spoon in the apple mixture. (If you are too energetic, the whole thing will go flat.)
Now pour the mixture into little glass dishes and put a blob of red jam on the top.

Charles says you could use apricot or pear sauce instead of apple, for a change.

17

Knickerbocker Glory

Enough for 4 people

3 packets of jello, red, green and yellow

fresh fruit – an orange, raspberries, grapes, bananas, etc, *or* 1 can of mixed fruit

a few drops of lemon juice

1 block of ice cream (your favorite flavor)

glacé cherries (2)

a chocolate flake } for decoration

whipped cream

Find 4 long thin glasses.

If you are using fresh fruit, peel it, take out the pips etc, and cut it up into spoon-sized pieces. Now sprinkle it with a few drops of lemon juice. If you are using canned fruit, drain off the juice, first. It can be used as part of the liquid when making the jello.

Next, get someone to help you make the three kinds of jello and divide the fruit between them, saving a few pieces for decoration. Put the jello in a cool place to set.

Then put one tablespoon of the red jello at the bottom of each glass. Next put in a spoonful of ice cream. Then put in a layer of green jello and another spoonful of ice cream, followed by a layer of yellow jello and so on until you are nearly at the top of each glass.

Now put in a few of the pieces of fruit
 you have saved and a large spoonful
 of ice cream.
Decorate as you like with flaked
 chocolate, nuts and halved glacé
 cherries. A whirl of cream on top
 looks especially good.

Real lemonade

Enough for 4 people

4 lemons
$2\frac{1}{4}$ cups of sugar
1 pint of boiling water
1 tablespoon of honey

Take off the yellow part of the lemon
  with a potato-peeler, leaving the
  bitter white pith.
Put the rind in a heat-proof pitcher
  and add the sugar and honey. Now
  get someone to pour on the boiling
  water for you. Stir to dissolve the
  sugar and then leave until it is cool.
Next, squeeze the juice from the
  lemons and add to the mixture in
  the pitcher.
Finally, pour the lemonade through
  a sieve to strain off the rind.
Fill each glass about half full, add
  water to taste and as many ice
  cubes as will fit.
This lemonade has a delicious fruity
  taste and is not acid at all.

Louise says, do you know how to
make *Ice Cream Soda*? Simply add a
large scoop of ice cream and a big
straw to a glassful of your favorite
fizzy drink.

20

Creamy milk shake

William says, if you are feeling like something long and cool and creamy, then there is nothing quite like your own milk shake.

½ pint of milk
4 tablespoons ice cream (your favorite flavor)
½ cherry – for each person

Put the milk and half the ice cream (about 2 tablespoons) into a large, glass screw-top jar. Screw the top on tight, then shake the jar until the mixture is thick and frothy and then pour into 2 tall glasses.
Add a tablespoon of ice cream to each glass. Now put as big a straw as you can find into each glass and ½ a cherry on the ice cream.
This makes a very creamy milk shake. If you like a stronger flavor, add a squeeze of fruit syrup to the milk before you shake it.

Bear's hot chocolate

Enough for 3 people

1 pint of milk
1 tablespoon of chocolate powder
2 tablespoons of honey (runny honey is best)

Mix the chocolate powder, honey and 1 tablespoon of milk together in a heat-proof pitcher until they are creamy and smooth.
Then get someone to warm the rest of the milk and pour it into the pitcher. Stir until everything is well mixed and pour into three mugs.

21

Triple-decker sandwiches

Or, the best things come in threes

John says choose fillings with different colors. It's odd, but it seems to make them taste nicer.

3 slices of brown or white bread from a large loaf
   (try using both)
softened butter for spreading
2 different sorts of filling

Spread one of the fillings on a slice of buttered bread and then put another slice on top.
Next, put in a different kind of filling and finally put your third slice on top of this. Be careful not to spread on too much filling, or it will squeeze out everywhere.
Now cut the bread firmly in four.

Fillings

Egg and Cheese

1 hard-boiled egg
pepper
1 tablespoon of grated cheese
1 tablespoon of mayonnaise
a teaspoon of softened butter

Mash up the hard-boiled egg with a fork and add grated cheese, butter and mayonnaise. Mix everything up as well as you can, add a dash of pepper and it is ready to spread.
Sara says that if the spread looks a little dry, add a few drops of single cream to make it more creamy.

Tuna fish mayonnaise

1 small can of tuna fish
2 tablespoons of mayonnaise
pinch of salt and pepper
a few drops of lemon juice

Open the can and then drain off the oil from the
fish. Next, simply mix everything together in a
bowl to a soft paste.

Tomato and Lettuce

1 large firm tomato
2 small lettuce leaves
salt and pepper

Wash the lettuce leaves and shake off the extra
water before you put them on the bread. Slice the
tomato and add a little salt and pepper. Put the
tomato on the lettuce.

Grated cheese and chutney

1 tablespoon grated cheese
1 teaspoon of chutney or sweet pickle

Mix these two together to a paste.

Cream cheese and sliced cucumber

Cream cheese and chopped pineapple
or chopped, stoned dates

Louise says that for all these cream cheese recipes,
you could use grated or cottage cheese instead.
Always spread on the cheese first before you add
the fruit.

Cottage cheese and sliced apricots

Sliced banana and peanut butter

23

A bear's own cookies

2 cups plain flour
4 oz butter or margarine
$\frac{1}{2}$ cup sugar
1 tablespoon of milk
1 tablespoon of honey (runny honey is best)
1 egg yolk (if you have it)
currants ⎫
glacé cherries ⎬ for decoration

Oven setting:
350°F

Turn on the oven.
Mix the butter or margarine, sugar, and honey together in a
   bowl until they are smooth and creamy.
Sift the flour into the bowl, add the milk and mix everything
   firmly together until it makes a stiff dough.
Sprinkle the table with a little flour, and roll out your dough
   until it is about $\frac{1}{4}$ inch (5 mm) thick.
Now draw a bear on a piece of paper and cut it out. Lay the
   paper on the dough and cut the dough round it.
   Do this as many times as you can. (You can make other
   shapes with the left-over dough.) Stick on currants for eyes,
   and a piece of glacé cherry for the nose.
With a spoon or pastry brush, lightly coat the bears with egg
   yolk and slide them onto a greased oven tin. Bake them in
   the oven for about 12–15 minutes, or until they are a pale
   golden brown.
Leave to cool for about 10 minutes. It is worth waiting because
   these cookies will not be crisp until they have cooled.

24

25

 # Mooncake

4 oz softened butter or margarine
½ cup soft brown sugar
½ teaspoon vanilla
1 egg – well beaten
½ teaspoon baking soda
½ teaspoon salt
8 oz bar plain or cooking chocolate
  chopped into pea-sized pieces
1½ cups plain flour

Oven setting:
  350°F

Turn on the oven.
Beat the butter or margarine, sugar
  and vanilla together in a large bowl
  until the mixture looks like thick
  cream. Now add the egg, and mix
  again.
Next sift together flour, salt and
  baking soda and carefully stir it
  into the butter and egg mixture.
  Don't be too energetic, or your
  cake will tend to be soggy.
Mix in the chopped chocolate, and
  then scrape the gooey mixture into
  a buttered sponge tin so that it is
  about ½ an inch (10 mm) thick.
  Don't forget to grease the tin, or
  your cake will stick.
Bake for 30 minutes. Then turn out of
  the tin and leave to cool.

26

Frosting

If you want to frost your Mooncake . . .

$\frac{2}{3}$ cup confectioners sugar

2 oz softened butter

2 tablespoons of orange or lemon
   juice

Beat the butter until creamy and then
   little by little add the sugar and
   juice. Keep on beating until the
   mixture is smooth, and spoon onto
   the cake.

Now you can decorate with Moon
   decorations – shiny silver balls, or
   sugar sweets, or colored sprinkles.

27

Crunchy celery dip

4 oz of cream cheese
3 tablespoons of single cream
1 tablespoon of chopped celery
pinch of pepper (paprika is nice)
2 teaspoons mayonnaise

Put the cheese in a bowl, add the cream
and mayonnaise and beat until the
mixture is smooth and creamy.
Add the pepper and the chopped
celery and spoon into a dish.
Now you can eat it with crisps, thin
sticks of carrot or cheese biscuits.

Sara says you could use 1 tablespoon
of chopped pineapple, or chopped
apple instead of the celery.

Celery trees

2 sticks of celery
a glass of ice-cold water

Cut two sticks of celery into pieces
about twice as long as your finger.
Now make several cuts lengthwise
right through the celery to about an
inch from the bottom and put them
into the glass of ice-cold water.
Leave them for about an hour. The
thin strips you have cut in the
celery will curl back and make the
sticks look like little trees.

Toasted cheese boats

For 4 people

4 large potatoes
a little cooking oil
8 heaping tablespoons of grated cheese
4 tablespoons single cream
2 oz butter
salt and pepper
4 pieces of celery, about as long as
   your finger

Oven setting:
  350°F

Turn on the oven.
Scrub the potatoes, and cut out any black marks. Now rub
   them with cooking oil and put them on a baking tray in the
   oven for 1½ hours.
Take them out of the oven, split them open and scoop out the
   insides into a mixing bowl. (Remember, they will be hot!)
   Next add half of the grated cheese, single cream, butter,
   pepper and salt (go easy on the salt, because the cheese is
   salty already), and mix everything up with a fork.
Spoon the mixture into the potato shells, sprinkle what is left
   of the grated cheese on top, and put the shells back in the
   oven for 10 minutes or so, or until the top looks golden brown
   and crunchy.
Take them out of the oven, and stick a piece of celery firmly
   into each shell to make the mast of your boat.
Now you can eat them!

Something that looks exciting at parties, is easy to make and very nice to eat is:

Frosted fruit

fruit – red apples, pears, plums, grapes, orange segments
1 egg white
4 tablespoons of sugar

Find some fruit and polish it until it is colorful and shiny. If you use orange segments, be careful not to split the skin because the sharp juice will melt the frosting.

Now, put the sugar in a flat dish. Put the egg white in a bowl (see *A bear's own cookies* for ideas to use the yolks), and whip it lightly until it is frothy but not stiff.

Next, dip each piece of fruit carefully in the egg white. It is a good idea to paint on the egg white with a pastry brush, if you have one.

Now roll the fruit lightly in sugar and arrange on a large, flat dish.

When you have finished, put the dish in a cool place, so that the frosting can harden.

Eat the same day.

The party was over.
Charles was already planning
their *next* one.

Then Fred yawned;
it *was* time for bed.